UPDATE ON THE DESCENT

Ellen Hinsey was born in 1960. For the last twenty years she has lived and traveled in Europe, witnessing firsthand the fall of the Berlin Wall and other events. She is the author of *Update on the Descent*, a 2007 National Poetry Series Finalist (Bloodaxe Books, 2009), *The White Fire of Time* (Wesleyan University Press, 2002/Bloodaxe Books, 2003) and *Cities of Memory*, which was awarded the Yale University Series Prize. She has also edited and translated *The Junction: Selected Poems of Tomas Venclova* (Bloodaxe Books, 2008). Her poems, essays and translations have appeared in many publications including *The New York Times*, *The New Yorker*, *Poetry Review*, *Poetry* and *The Irish Times*. Selections of her work have appeared in French, Italian, German, Danish and Serbian translation. Her translations of contemporary French fiction and memoir are published with Riverhead/Penguin Books. Among other honours, she has been the recipient of a Rona Jaffe Foundation Writer's Award, a Berlin Prize Fellowship from the American Academy in Berlin and a Lannan Foundation Award. She lives in Paris.

Update on the Descent is the companion volume to *The White Fire of Time*, which was written following a tragedy in the poet's family. *The White Fire of Time* is a reflection on the *Vita Contemplativa*, or the contemplative life. *Update on the Descent* combines personal experience with research carried out at an international tribunal. A modern *Vita Activa*, it is a meditation on the extremes of the human condition.

ELLEN HINSEY

UPDATE
ON THE DESCENT

BLOODAXE BOOKS

ISBN: 978 1 85224 833 8

First published 2009 by
Bloodaxe Books Ltd,
Highgreen,
Tarset,
Northumberland NE48 1RP.

www.bloodaxebooks.com
For further information about Bloodaxe titles
please visit our website or write to
the above address for a catalogue.

Bloodaxe Books Ltd acknowledges
the financial assistance of
Arts Council England, North East.

Typesetting by Jean-Marc Eldin

Cover design: Neil Astley & Pamela Robertson-Pearce

Printed in Great Britain by
Bell & Bain Limited, Glasgow, Scotland

Language is punishment. All things must enter into language and remain there according to the degree of their guilt.

INGEBORG BACHMANN

The unheard of has become everyday.

INGEBORG BACHMANN

Contents

Acknowledgments

Grateful acknowledgment is made to the following periodicals, in which selections of this work have previously appeared:

Poetry:
  "Interdiction"
  "Update on the Last Judgment"

Poetry Review:
  "A Short Primer on Imagination and Destruction"

The New England Review:
  "Report on the Descent"
  "Transcript"

Agni Review:
  "Aphorisms Regarding Impatience"

The Southwest Review:
  "On Things Remembered in Innocence"
  (Awarded the *2007 Stover Prize by the Southwest Review*)

Poetry Ireland:
  "On the Singular Instant of Now"

The Missouri Review:
  "Inventory"
  "Testimony on What is Important"
  "A Concise Biography of Tyranny"

Jubilat:
  "Notebook C: On the Discomfort of Being in Time"

Conjunctions:
  "Notebook A: Notes on Wakefulness and Being"

Poetry International:
  "A Natural History of Compassion"

The Los Angeles Review:
  "An Intimate History of the Hand"

The Warwick Review:
  "Twelve Reflections on Renewal"

The Cuirt Annual of the Galway International Festival of Literature:
  "A Brief Review of Suppositions"

The Wolf Magazine:
  "On the Midnight Dialogue with History"

Ars Interpres:
  "Notebook B: On Place and the Territory of the Other"

Some of these poems also appeared in translation:

Siècle 21 / translated into French by Anne Talvaz:
  "Interdiction"

Poesia e Spiritualità / translated into Italian by Roberto Lombardo:
  "Notebook B: On Place and the Territory of the Other"

Akzente / translated into German by Maja Ueberle-Pfaff and Uta Gosmann:
  "A Concise Biography of Tyranny"
  "A Short Primer on Imagination and Destruction"
  "A Brief Review of Suppositions"
  "Testimony on What is Important"
  "Interdiction"

Kritik / translated into Danish by Jens-Martin Eriksen:
  "Transcript"
  "Inventory"
  "Testimony on What is Important"
  "A Concise Biography of Tyranny"

Književni Magazin / translated into Serbian by Djordje Krivokapic:
  "A Concise Biography of Tyranny"
  "Update on the Last Judgment"

*For its support during the time this book was written,
the author would like to thank The American Academy in Berlin.*

PART ONE

THE HUMAN ELEMENT

I.

Historiae

ON THE SINGULAR INSTANT OF NOW

I.

In that first hour, balanced on the edge of darkness,

　　　　When, without loss, the *now* unwraps its light—

In that very first instant—horizon of unmade honey,

　　　　Oracle, unformed being—on that singular edge

II.

Of day, when the *new* arises, and with insistent force

　　　　Undoes the realm of *nothing*—when that very

First moment arrives, erasing shadow, bringing fresh

　　　　Warmth to poplar, decaying oak, ropes of ivy—

Effacing night dreams held in the roots of the arbor—

III.

In that moment, on that edge, from that realm which

　　　　Lifts potential into *being*—so that the actual

Approaches, nears embodiment; so that, at that exact

        Impress of light *everything ignites*: the bare

Awkwardness of birch, the sour sturdiness of pine,

        Grasses still heaped up, hills pinned in frost—

IV.

The spied-out homes of wasps deep in the river's bank,

        The outskirts of fog-bound cities, water rat trails—

All renewed in that sudden epiphany: that sudden rage

        Of enduring renewal—issued from unique silence

And blind continuation—when the energy of that first

        Intention beats its pulse down on all that is coming,

V.

All that is known—and the waiting, rough world forms

        Again, carving itself out of the seeds of *before*—

Until all flares: in that *first, last, eternal* burst of *Now*—

        Then Day, sovereign, surveys its realms, finds

Old minerals thawing in earth: then—when all that

        Can be said starts to form in the mouth—rises

VI.

In the mind, races along the known paths of thought:
>   There—faced by that possibility, which is forever

Hostage to every unpredictable hour of *after*—What
>   Shall we call it, how shall we describe its Nature?

In that instant of uncertain illumination and mystery
>   Of purpose, in what true language, new or ancient—

Can we speak of the grief of its squandered promise?

II.

Correspondences

AN INTIMATE HISTORY OF THE HAND

I.
Condition

About the Hand, nothing has changed. When its moment comes, it is deferential and compliant.

2.
Nature

Yet, despite its mindlessness, it is always convinced of its righteous authority.

3.
Genesis

It lifts each time out of the primordial wood—enveloped in the scent of barbarous necessity.

4.
Understanding

It is swiftly assuaged of guilt. The raised Hand is a catalogue of justifications.

5.
Sympathy

And the Body, in agreement, is easily lifted beneath it.

6.
Inspiration
It is fearless and bold, but nevertheless draws, if it must, from History's trove of notorious gestures.

7.
Method
The Hand, thus emboldened, imagines to derive strength from Hector's ceaseless blows.

8.
Comment
The Hand's logic has always been fed by suspect mythologies.

9.
Means
The Hand appreciates convenience: a stone or club fits nicely.

10.
Intention
But the Hand loves best the close, direct blow. There it can witness the blood rise, and the eyes close.

11.
Apologia
The Hand's secret impotence has always been assuaged by blood's signature, scrawled before it on the ground.

(a)

"Nature… how surpassing the intelligence, how vast the resources…"

III.

Annals

A NATURAL HISTORY OF COMPASSION

{Exhibit A}

There, in the twenty-fourth chapter—embedded in archaic vowels like coiled fossils found in clay—one finds the story of how, after the toiling of war, when enemies finally lay together in the dust, in that hour when the bereaved search out a place where sorrow can rest, the old king yoked together the sharp-hoofed mules, and parting all in attendence, lashed the startled horses on—

And drove through the opened city gates into night's uncertain province—

And how, from on high, a swift messenger was sent to close the enemy's eyes in sleep, so that the king might travel unseen and bring his mission to completion. And how, awake in his rough-hewn lodge, within hearing's distance of the beaked ships, the great warrior—who, for nine days in his own grief had wept—there received him;

And how, to his own amazement, before the towering shoulders, the old king bent down, and in broken sorrow for his son, kissed the hand of the one who had slain him;

And how the warrior, watchful of the pain he bore, in sudden compassion took hold of the old man's wrists, and in words drawn up from grief's sharp abyss, vowed to return his son's body—even in its lifelessness. And how, there, side by side, in night's closed vault, in a commonality of breath and skin, the two mature men wept—each for his own.

While under each word the ceaseless river of revenge flowed.

NOTEBOOK A

IV.

Notebook A

NOTES ON WAKEFULNESS AND BEING

{a.}

Origins

The body resists its knowledge of *oneness*—as if to exist it must renounce that from which it was issued.

As a child believes it must deny its origins in order to affirm its singular existence.

It is not possible to deviate from *being*.

Intention

The body insists on its singular song: the melody of a reed in a gale.

At the Same Time

The basso-continuo of *being* roils in the marrow of all matter.

Paradoxical Given

Not all felicitious insights can be harvested from the garden of the world.

Particularity

Inherently Problematic
To imagine an escape from *being* through a flight into *particularity*.

Addendum
To champion *particularity* is to always remain suspicious of one's true nature.

The Dilemna
What is *particular* is like Narcissus leaning over the water's reflection, eternally hoping, but never assuredly able to confirm, the existence of his singular beauty.

Beyond the Edge of the Garden
To believe one is hunted by *manifestation*, hounded by *particularity*—

Fortunate Parallels
The green flame of cypress, the hoarfrost of fern—the many-sided argument of the raspberry thicket.

Postulate
In order to fully make peace with *being* one must first make peace with the *vanity of particularity*.

Unexplainable Grief

To witness, at Autumn's end, the fallen walnut broken into its parts.

Hidden Grief

The brain's twin hemispheres halving *continuity* into *discontinuity*.

What is Difficultly Visualized

Dualities that shelter behind them a unity beyond the possibility of conceptual formation.

Insights Beyond the Realm of Thought

Twilight-colored plums, fallen but luminous, hidden among the autumn grass.

Almost Observable by the Naked Eye

Being's armature holding up all that is starkly ephemeral.

Insight and Doubt

To experience, even once, the unexpected unity of the world— pitted against the shadowy machinations of the Mind.

{d.}

Assault

Enduring Condition
Wakefulness invites the Mind to join with it in the world's
burgeoning, always-renewing field.

Curious Auto-da-fé
In return, the Mind plots its eternal assault on *being*.

The Covert Habits of the Mind
Like bats winging through the shadowy, damp night orchard.

A Question of Methodology
To *unthink* the mind's habits in a gesture of sympathy with
being.

Intuitive Postulate
Insight opens its reticent blossoms when the Mind waits under
the same sky as *Wakefulness*.

Unfortunate Parallel
Human hair and blood—matted like dank manure and straw.

Goal of Difficult Attainment

To remain on the threshold of: *particularity, oneness* and *language*—to negotiate along the joints of the world.

Unattainable Ideal

Perfect Wakefulness, like the moon ever-visible at midday.

Urgent Dilemma

To resolve how that which is both *same* and *different* can finally be called by its singular, Sacred name.

Return

Hence the implicit *homecoming* of metaphor: to reconcile what was arbitrarily broken, exiled in the mind.

Drawback

The Will listens in on all the manifestations of wonder.

Wakefulness and Surprise

To listen along the joints—for all that surprisingly joins.

V.

Testimony

A BRIEF REVIEW OF SUPPOSITIONS

It is enough that Time pierces us with its iron.

That the body—weary cargo of flesh—must lay down each
Night at darkness's ancient threshold.

It is enough that envy breeds like rust in still water;
That knowledge can be effaced as easily as script on a wall's
Exposed façade.

That a solitary lament can rise, but remain alone—isolated as before
The violent indifference of the earth.
Or that evening,

Already so darkly grasped,
Can be intimately penetrated by a violence of blood and
Sperm.

That the animal prowls in our veins. That in the eye lurks
The pitiless spider.

Or that the mouth, stubborn witness to being, refuses to learn
The common vowels of *forgiveness*—

Is it not enough that this body, wooden burden of hopes, yields
To the eternal kingdoms of *time, mass, gravity*—

That a hand, raised purposefully—or with indifference—can
Bring the body of another to a crouch—

Or that, by the blow of mere inflicted hunger, all the words
Of the Scriptures can be erased?

So that, what is lowly, can be made more lowly still?

(b)
"It is this perfectibility manifested in nature…"

VI.

Correspondences

INVENTORY OF BELIEFS REGARDING INSTINCT

1.

Definition

Instinct is only a part of the overall composition of human nature.

2.

Clarification

Instincts are not generally defined as either "good" or "bad".

3.

Bibliography

Certain nineteenth-century works concluded the final domestication of instinct.

4.

Agrarian Thesis

Instinct now has a quiet mountain pasture, where it cultivates crops in accordance with the seasons.

5.

Proof Pending

For some time now, instinct has been on its best behavior.

6.
Scope
Instinct is principally concerned with private functions related to the body and the appetite.

7.
Personal Hygiene
Instinct cleans up after itself.

8.
Perception
Instinct has no knowledge of the movement of things, such as troops and international monetary funds.

9.
Syntax
A neutral phrase: *"In the final analysis, I acted instinctively."*

10.
Mystery
Instinct is as puzzled as the rest of us about the existence of secret military prisons and mass graves.

11.
Two Hypotheses
a) Instinct listens to reason. *b)* Instinct and reason are still on speaking terms.

12.
Only a Rumor
Instinct is not plotting its ultimate triumph.

VII.

Chronicle

PREPARATION FOR THE DESCENT

{Cantos I–XXII}

To begin—take the path at the edge of the ancient wood.

There, before you, will be the blighted, gnarled trees that bend and indicate the way forward, if it is forward.

The shadowy path will open among dusky roots: brambles threaded with thorny leaves—or poisonous weeds sewn among flinty stones.

And seized by its own sudden thunder of heart-beat—surging, inner toiling of cell, your body will fear and cause you to stumble—

But don't hesitate—press determinedly along, until you reach where unimaginable vistas open beneath blackening, granite skies,

And the final descent appears where the fading light glows.

There, rising up from that forbidding, oppressive air, you will hear the anguished voices of lament: the wrathful, twisting in the abysmal sea's flames; or the violent—forever naked, scourged beneath the bludgeoning rains.

Know that the road will be hard. The descent will be deep.

In the torch-light of that heat, turn your face from those consumed by pain—those scalded by blood; in your brief passage there indulge neither your curiosity, nor your pity.

Continue until you can't advance further; raise your eyes up to the mountainside's light. To that rugged incline that was once said to lead up to Paradise.

But, you have read this before. From the start, you have known you can always just turn the page.

The real journey is stranger: the one through which we are never led.

Our everyday descent into the human element.

PART TWO

Testimony

VIII.

Historiae

ON THINGS REMEMBERED IN INNOCENCE

I.

The damp, fragrant fields were verdant with possibility—

    A lamp's shifting flame provided solace before sleep,

The land endured—sustained by its own rough necessity,

    While renewal grew in the granite well and flourished

II.

As night deposited star-seed in its deep, fertile waters.

    A stone wall divided only familiar shadows at dayfall;

The white of daylily co-existed with lichen's decay.

    A footstep was erased only by the wind's unknowing—

While the taciturn threat of storm never outweighed

III.

The eternal dream of summer. Bees' honey thickened

    In rock crevices, overflowed the milky edge of day.

The unknown of distance brought no need for alarm.
                    The dark muscle of bales remained lifeless on the fields.

A furrow's length was measured only by a day's labor,
                    While the far-off hills concealed only dusk, wild ravens,

IV.

Blue sage, white clover—all erased in twilight's eclipse.
                    Midnight was populated merely by the innocence of sleep.

A raised hand was silenced by the just shield of a word.
                    The woodshed's dark did not fear the blue-sharpened blade.

Blind cumulus carried prayers over bright fields of rape,
                    And when the winds rose, visited roofs, rattled dry thatch—

V.

The heart did not turn, grow black in anxious wonder.
                    Lime's whiteness had not imagined a mouth's open grave.

Noon was heralded only by a lizard's mottled armor,
                    A river's turbulent waters still reconciled opposing shores—

The voice did not ask *why?* but *how to justly praise it*—
                    And when the fiery hour of dusk fell, the air filled only

VI.

With the sudden agitated smoke of starling's restlessness.
> In each village, strange courted strange and embraced it.

Languages frequented each other's houses, raised a glass.
> For what *did not exist*, did not anticipate its conception,

And what had *not yet been done* need not seek redemption,
> And private grief still held to its just, proper proportions—

For out of shared night—day still patiently remade the world.

IX.

Correspondences

TRANSCRIPT

1.

Why was the language of the other forbidden?
Because daylight had always risen equally above the houses.

2.

How did you know the enemy?
By the similarity of birth, marriage, all the rites of passage.

3.

Why were the crops destroyed in the fields?
Because they had always been shared abundance and staff.

4.

What were the words the other spoke?
Today, I rise for washing. Today, I labor first light to last.

5.

Why was the land divided into homeland and territory?
Because ravens nested *here* by the river, *there* in rain-soaked oaks.

6.

Why were the men separated from the women?

Because life is endurance; because love eases the labor of dailiness.

7.

Why were the villages laid to waste?

Because time must be sheltered—because it requires a sanctity of place.

8.

Why were the well waters left unclean?

Because shared waters must be clear; because not everything can be restored by prayer.

9.

Why were the walls smeared with blood?

Because the body contains final knowledge—which even in its brokenness cannot be undone.

10.

Who said to shoot without mercy?

Because the hand remembers, knows it must face the soul.

11.

And who said that darkness can triumph?

Because of the ravens, the river, the torched grain: because of the slaughtered Word.

(c)

"When the illogical became the ferryman of the dead…"

X.

Annals

INVENTORY

Preparation

This is a room that you cannot just enter. *This is a room that is not empty.* You must wait at the threshold. *It was once a house, a schoolroom, a factory.* Now there is no window glass, and the branches of the bare trees refuse to touch the sills. *You must wait at the threshold.* Inside, it is freezing. There are four walls, a wide crack in the plaster. The cement floor will never be repaired. It holds what imagination cannot. *It was once a factory, a schoolroom, a house.* What remains is evidence. What has been lost is evidence. This is a room you cannot just enter.

Inventory

1. The body doesn't need much at the end. A bit of wood, a white cloth.
    A small shelter for its passing.

2. Here, lined up head to head, and foot to foot, is life's inventory.
    This one was a husband. This one was a brother.

3. The white room is ablaze with a stunned wakefulness.
   Forgive those who trespass against—

4. Don't stare at the faces doing their death-work.
   It is a type of sacrilege...

5. Don't imagine the dead are at peace.
   The dead are at your mercy.

6. And what is that silence which is not, could never be,
   mere silence?
   This is a room that you cannot just enter.

NOTEBOOK B

XI.

Notebook B

ON PLACE AND THE TERRITORY OF THE OTHER

I.

{The Unquantifiable}

The vine, ridge and field are unquantifiable. They are only themselves.

The Self in landscape is a contradiction: implies a state of homelessness that can never be healed.

Eternal Dilemma
The Self in its nakedness is untenable—a mystery.

Regarding the Search for Identity
The Self founders in self-definition like an animal in muddy water. Little adheres, most washes off.

The Self, in its poverty, shores up its house using the struts of the radical Will.

Disquieting Hypothesis
Where the Self ends, the myth of origins begins.

II.

{Origins}

Simple Postulate

That which must be protected by the sword implies dissenting claims.

Not a Tautology

Only that which is incontestable can be considered Absolute.

Regarding Chapter and Verse

After Adam and Eve's envy of God's knowledge, the Self's belief in *birthright* was its most perilous sin.

Common Exegesis

Birthright is the failure of the Self to accept the *placeless* nature of being.

De Facto

Only the Absolute sleeps at night without the fear of the ancient, bloody sword.

Uncomfortable Thesis

The Tribe, in itself, is not holy.

III.

{Terra}

Under the Sign of Mars
The Tribe is ever alert to *difference*, which it exalts to a *cult of possibility*.

Contributing Variable
The origins of *difference* always reach back to the radical Will of the self.

While in Essence
The Tribe requires *the other* to determine the frontiers of its own poverty.

Elementary, but Dangerous Given
The Tribe, unable to conclusively possess *place*, must invent a mythology of homeland born out of the *happenstance of earth*.

Not a Paradox
The *cult of difference* is always the grave of the Self.

Unexpected Encounter
The Tribe is ever surprised before the *other's* broken body—by the eternal *sameness* of its blood.

{Matter and Will}

Metaphysical Review
The most radical forms of Will are always the compromise of *spirit* for *matter*.

Genesis of Will
The *matter* of the Will is formed out of the evasive, gaseous universe of the Mind.

Astronomical Factor
Radical Will always engenders a form of eclipse.

Simple Supposition
If Evil exists, it cannot be separated from its origins in the self.

Theorem of Grief
Evil does not exist: only the eclipse that radical Will casts across the face of God.

In Memoriam
Those singular acts of Will whose chaos pulls the world back to its black roots.

V.

{Final Borders}

Ideal Absolute
The Self must be divested of its longing for place to regain its
essence.

Mythologies Concerning Territory
Like a haze at midday that obscures the patent visibility of
eternal *temporality*.

Optimistic Postulate
Despite its homelessness, the Self can find sanctuary in the
eternal *Now*—the ever-renewing instant of *world* and *other*.

Archaic Psalm
Where you go, stranger, I shall go, flesh of my flesh.

In the Light of Time
Where each one goes—through the valley of the earth,
surrounded by the low, darkening hills and thick, ivory sky—

There are no boundaries: traversed as it is by the terrible and
merciless waters of *common being*.

XII.

Testimony

TESTIMONY ON WHAT IS IMPORTANT

I.

I am only telling you what I have heard.
He said that he was in a room, on a yellow tiled floor. There were men,
And familiar voices.

On the floor of the room was a bucket of water.
He only regained consciousness when his head was pulled out of it.

II.

They kicked him until he defecated and his body failed.
He couldn't walk then,
Or urinate for a week. *Beyond the door there were men and familiar voices.*

On the floor was a bucket of water.
He apologized to the court, because what he had to say next

III.

Was "obscene". *"I am sorry to those present,"* He said,
As if obscenity can be forgiven.
They forced his genitals into another man's mouth. Then, voicelessly,

Tried to set them on fire.
The court questioned him, said, *"We are only interested in the facts."*

IV.

He said, *"But, I have something to add—"*
"Something important." He said he knew the torturer. He knew the man.
And while, voicelessly, these acts

Were carried out, he asked the man if he knew what he was doing. On *fire*—
He said, *"Do you know what you are doing?"* The court said, *"Stick to the facts."*

V.

The man said, *"But this is what is important."* He said
He asked the man: *"Do you know what you are doing?"* He said the man
Did not answer. He said, *"I have to say this: this is what is important."*

(d)

"Do not hold it against me, O speech…"

XIII.

Correspondences

A SHORT PRIMER ON IMAGINATION
AND DESTRUCTION

1.

Prima Facie

Not every act, performed in hostage to the mind, can be contained in language.

2.

Lexicology

That which exists on the periphery of language is a shade; forced to wander eternally in a terror of disclosure.

3.

Transmission

What remains unspoken in consciousness passes, like a form of inheritance, into the estate of common being.

4.

Perplexing Paradox

That which eludes language exerts an impossible weight on the center of speech.

5.

Cause and Effect

Heraclitus believed that, in the end, all matter would be burned in the crux of time.

6.
Fallible Corollary

That which resists being revealed must one day be burned up in utterance.

7.
Paradox of Grief

To speak is an impossible form of renewal. *What has been done cannot be restored by language.*

To speak is essential to affirm the *potential of utterance*, which is its own capital.

8.
Battle Report

In obscure night he fell, his entrails spilled, his blood filling the furrows of earth dark red.

9.
Regnum Imaginarii

Imagination is subject to its own sovereign laws: not all that is executed can be *imagined*.

10.
House of Death

Clawing the dust, life was torn from him—and the weight of hateful darkness closed in.

11.
Petrification

The imagination, stunned, drew its shield up against the contorted writhings of the mind.

12.
Nunc et Semper

Do not speak of it—it was unimaginable.

XIV.

Chronicle

A CONCISE BIOGRAPHY OF TYRANNY

Tyranny does not mind starting out small: it is indifferent to scale. Its dreams of grandeur are happily rehearsed in a child's theatre.

There, Tyranny has a full set of tin soldiers with which to prepare a catastrophe. One wears a gas mask; another a metal helmet. Hidden in a drawer, away from the others, is the drummer whose head has been blown off.

Tyranny has an awkward adolescence: it's all arms and legs and hot air. It talks of keeping the streets clean, while it fills them with a litter of noise.

Tyranny likes to have a hometown—and a small cinema where its faithful can watch films in the evenings.

Tyrannies learn slowly: it is only in young adulthood that they acquire the true benefits of decorum. They then possess the ability to carry out their work like any proper business.

In maturity, Tyranny becomes a *bona fide* adult—endowed with a fully-grown body—behind which it conceals a warehouse of regression.

Tyranny's regression is simple: an infant's desire to impose its omnipotence on the world.

Tyrannies are not good at aging. Tyrannies stay fit on a challenge. The thrill is lost when all the brave are dead.

Tyranny in old age is never graceful. Surrounded by rusted cars and old foundries, it is a junk heap of promises.

And as in Roman times, its successor was already, years ago, slain.

The mystery is why one finds, time and again, flowers on its grave.

PART THREE

MIDNIGHT DIALOGUE

XV.

Historiae

ON THE MIDNIGHT DIALOGUE WITH HISTORY

I.

Night without moon. Come closer—the gardens are blooming
Grey under the darkness. High above, the heavens waver,

In their frozen atmosphere. An ancient shape approaches—
Is there a voice? No voice, but something trembles deeply

II.

In the obscurity. Nearby, the shadows knit together rough
Pines, hiding the furtive night of animals: foxes, rodents—

The spilled entrails of the simple field mouse. Movements
Invade the thick silence—rustle in the hedge by the edge

Of the shadowy well, under the anxious grey sleep of owls—

III.

Turn now and take stock. On the shoulder of the road where
The grit of rain washes sand down to ditches. Wait. Listen—

For this approach: nearing with its vast inventory of trials and
          Events. *Rarely has it been so near*—this breath on your own

Breath, this immense, time-heavy weight. Far-off, the poplars
          Are a wave of black: then disquiet forces the dark to wake—

IV.

In this hour, when what rises from these penetrating streams
          Of damp demands to be known, to be owned—hold out your

Hand, so that, as if in chorus, the lost voices come, rising from
          The fissures of ruined, creviced walls: up from obscure depths

Figures slowly emerge, rise and blur—rise, then pass beyond
          The low branches of sodden trees. Silence. *A bell rings once*

V.

Through the cold atmosphere. But then, you know it was not
          Necessary to see the faces: you have seen them all already—

Passing from station to station; have heard the labored breaths,
          Have seen the torturer's notes, the scattered identity papers,

Have seen the shallow graves, by the roadside, so near to the
          Churches, near to the mosques, near to where in the dark

VI.

The simple field mouse lies. *Silence.* The sleepless bell closes
           The moment with its rusty tongue. What existed, exists—

And will remain. But what briefly edged the darkness trembles
           And fades. Night's road is empty. But perhaps it always

Was—turning round again, there remains spread before you
           The old shape. Even without the steady light of a moon—

You know—it could only ever have been your own shadow.

XVII.

Correspondences

APHORISMS REGARDING IMPATIENCE

I.

Mythologies of the End

Each century believing itself poised as if on the edge of time.

2.

The Meaning of Impatience

Restlessness in time. To imagine that which is not swiftly accomplished will never be fulfilled.

3.

Displaced Envy

Unable to initiate creation, or manage civilization: the drive to engineer *decreation* with perfection.

4.

Perplexing Instincts

The division of the spirit between advancement and abandon.

5.

The Attraction of the Apocalypse

To control with absolute certainty one thing. And for it to be the last.

6.

Fragile Vector

The intersection where civilization and perseverance meet.

7.

The Effort of Civilization

Miraculous labor. Each day Sisyphus rolling his rock uphill against the accidental nature of mankind.

8.

Not a Solution

To draw into question Sisyphus's task.

9.

Accepting Negative Inevitability

Intellectual sleepwalking. The ethical self abdicating *affirmation* for the temptation of *renunciation*.

10.

Deviant Logic

To reject contingencies of disaster. To glean *possibility* from the crevices of *improbability*.

11.

What is at Stake

The fragile geometry of the world held in hostage.

12.

Not the End

A type of grace: waiting in impatience to see that, from now until the far edge of always, *nothing happens.*

(e)

"In what tense shall we now speak about the present?..."

XVII.

Annals

EASTERN APOCRYPHA

Night, Warsaw

It's sundown. August harvests its final hours: the air thick with industrial haze. The wilderness of dusk settled in white dust. Out from the railroad station bodies unwind, unravel, worn threads cut off from understandable fate. They spin out—refuse from the century's end. They bargain, buy currency, exchange needles, angst. The twilight deepens and drowns in evening torpor, and the station's orange light shines down like the jaundiced eye of God.

These individual trajectories—lines drawn from an obsolete compass: disorientation like a drug, like an eclipse. Half-lives in the mirrors of the public toilets, half-lives under the stained cardboard by the station. Distorted voices over loud speakers announce ultimate departures. There is momentary comfort in the pale lights and order of timetables. Then the late hour urges the bodies on—like water sweeping debris forward in drains.

Along the midnight boulevards, police cars cruise slowly to survey the pain. Ostentation flaunts with decay—but neither wins as night rolls up both in its worn carpet—to be hefted on the shoulders of weary sleepers, those innocent carriers of hope.

Somewhere, someone still remembers. Somewhere else, someone forgets.

Time, the impartial tyrant, grinds comprehension to oblivion: while long past midnight, towards the station, drift the night silhouettes. It's too late now to leave. Still, in slow motion towards the black mausoleum they come, as if caught for eternity in the underworld of the Passion's descent. But their eyes, animal-like in vapor-light, reflect an indestructible spark. Tomorrow there will still be a departure—sometime, for somewhere.

NOTEBOOK C

XVIII.

Notebook C

ON THE DISCOMFORT OF BEING IN TIME

{a.}

First Principles

Fate

Our first quandary is that our fate is the result of another's will.
To be willed into the world without our knowledge.

What is chosen can be *discarded;* what is not chosen must be
borne.

Addendum

Since life itself is never strictly *chosen*, it always bears the nature
of a pilgrimage.

Original Sin

Not to understand what crime we have committed to deserve our
discomfort.

Disquieting Solution

To seek out a temporary relief from *being's* discomfort through
Terror's release.

{b.}

Imperfection

Mistake

Evolution has seen to it that we can never quite grasp that life's imperfection is its condition *sine qua non*, and not an arbitrary mistake.

That life is lived like the two cities on Achilles' great shield: between the innocent joys of the wedding party—and the simple herdsmen murdered in the field.

That Life wills to undo itself by degrees—this incomprehensible betrayal.

Verticality

To be upright is to be wedged between imperfection and epiphany.

Ongoing Hope

That verticality can change the intrinsic nature of *being*—undo its lowly shuffling.

On the Contrary

Being-in-time is reigned over by its animality—its lumbering.

Passage

To *exist in time* is to pass though its eternal valley, encountering its many unconquerable furies—

The *fury of desire* that devours as it fulfils—like Prometheus
    chained to his fate;

The *fury of self-deception*—that separates the *self* from its own
    native element;

The *fury of progress*—that casts us out from living in the balm
    of time.

See Above

The Mind vaunts a singular passage through time, while—
aware of life's perpetual cycles—the lamenting mouth sprouts
its black orchids.

Late Knowledge

That suffering is a rare genus of flower that blooms on the
stalk of *being*.

Enduring Condition

The verb *to be* presents its choices: to bloom with Time or to
wantonly dig up the garden.

Multiplicity

Limitation

To be human is to come to terms with the fact that *being* discourages the experience of *sympathetic union*.

To never reside within the *intellect of ice*, the *just omnipotence of sunlight*, the *communal grace of water*.

To be singular: this obscure form of sorrow.

A Type of Challenge

To endure the perplexity of *being*—eternally poised between *singularity* and *oneness*—as if straddling the twin banks of a river that has no shores.

If Not, a Different Type of Arrival

To be at home for one moment in *insight*, as one would be in the four miraculous dimensions.

Addendum

To have a grasp of *oneness* is to be forever restless after its shadow.

Reconciliation

Envy

One comes to envy Sisyphus, for all his eternity and task: to understand one's fate fully, no matter how banal, and to be called to fulfill it with no fear of temporality.

Impossibility

To pause along the Pilgrimage's path, to halt in the constant gesture of *always-coming-into-being*.

Unexpected Release

Brief moments of respite: peace in the *chakra* of midday. Silence, the insects intent on their metallic swelling, the heat pressing down on each waxy leaf.

And for a moment, everything almost *in* it. Residing in the belly of it.

The Dream

To break open Time like a husk and examine its luminous, glowing seeds.

Naïve Theorem

Time, like gravity alone, is not sufficient to destroy us.

XIX.

Testimony

INTERDICTION

Ἀπόρρησις.

It is said that we can no longer use the old words.

Either, they carry in their script the imprint of our inhumanity:
The memory of the naked bodies burned as the classical strains played;

Or, contain their own blueprint of destruction: the way a seed
Harbors in its cells its final, latent corruption.

We have become afraid of them, the old words, as if at last we
Could escape punishment if, for once and for all, they were forbidden
Utterance in the public squares.

As if we could walk out to where the river joins that final deep,
Where the tides plow and reap the untouchable air. There beyond
Boundaries, voices.

Yet even where silence and the river Styx merge, there remain
Gestures that must be transcribed.

And I have listened to your voice at sundown, breaking with grief,
Undone by the bludgeoning tool of the eternal sorrows.

The way that Priam grieved, in the old words, the broken body
Of his son.

And heads are still brought openly to the market place, raised
As if in triumph.

The old words have blood on them.

But here, under the blackened sun, there are things, in the trammeled,
The ruined, the old words, which must still be said.

(f)
"The world is the closed door. It is a barrier. And at the same time it is the way through…"

XX.

Correspondences

TWELVE REFLECTIONS ON RENEWAL

1.

Quantum Postulate

Time, it has been proven, does not exist. Only *time* which lays in the wild obscurity beyond our conceptions.

2.

What Exists Nevertheless

The green dawn before memory. Consciousness's home in the origin of all things.

3.

Perplexing Forms of Animism

That concepts make their home in the *flesh of consciousness*, and, like all that is animate, must be *sustained*.

4.

Curiosité

That *levity of spirit* is sustained: despite the ensnaring gravity of the Mind's thicket.

5.

In Light Of

The undiminished instinct to target with violence—*the impulse to rise*.

6.

Taboo of Hope

The hushed consonant and supplicant vowel: suspended like the whisper of a spider across the lips.

7.

To be Ill at Ease with Events

When what *could be*, but never *should be*, crosses over the threshold of the imagination: *a trespassing of history*.

8.

What Must be Healed

The *traumas* of history, which preclude the possibility of the renewal of the spirit.

9.

Unproven Theorem

Contained in time is also the possibility of rebirth—a *forgiveness* of history.

10.

La Durée Difficile

The waiting that absolves memory and allows for forgiveness.

11.

Quantum Correction

Time would remake us in *its* image: fluid, and participants in the circular and unending path.

12.

Naïve Hypothesis

That the Spirit, digging deeper around the sunken weight of time, can find the way to *endure* and *flourish*.

XXI.

Chronicle

UPDATE ON THE LAST JUDGMENT

There will be no deafening noise. No hornblow of thunder.

The small plants of the earth will not tremble on the hillside as grace is prepared.

The sky will neither drown us in its plenty, nor the ground crack and consume feet in its hunger.

No, bodies will not, in their last rags of flesh, creep from under the earth, and with breath once torn from them, choke and expel the old mud of the world.

Adam and Eve, incredulous, will not embrace again in their poverty, not knowing whether to shield themselves or to emerge shameless from the past's shadow—astonished to again greet *terra firma*.

The book of the world, encrusted with deep-sea pearls and the blood of the lamb, will not open up its pages in which all deeds have been inscribed.

And the totality of history will not roll back together, all events fusing, once and for all, into the great blazing sphere of time.

None will sit on the right hand. There will be no right hand.

And the figure of sorrow and grace, with his staff upright, his purple pennant caught in that final wind, will not be there to greet us, with the mercy of justice in his eyes.

No, never Judgment. Just the abyss into which all acts are thrown down, and the terrible white silence in which judgment either endures or burns.

NOTES

Notes

The Human Element

(a) "Nature . . . how surpassing the intelligence, how vast the resources . . ." from Pliny the Elder, *The Natural History*, eds. John Bostock and H.T. Riley (London: 1855), XI.1.

"A Natural History of Compassion"

A 'natural history of compassion' poses the question of where our humanity comes from, how stable it is and whether it arises or can be claimed as part of our legacy as the human species. Robert Antelme writes of this in connection with the concentration camps of the twentieth century: *"Of the heroes we know about, from history or from literature…we do not believe that they were [ever able to express] as their last and only claim an ultimate sense of belonging to the human race. To say one felt oneself [in the camps] contested as a man, as a member of the human race . . . it was that that we felt most constantly and most immediately, and that—was what the others wanted."* Robert Antelme, *The Human Race* (Marlboro: Marlboro Press, 1992), 5-6.

(b) ". . . It is this perfectibility manifested in nature . . ." from Fabre d'Olivet, *The Golden Verses of Pythagoras* (New York: Solar Press, 1995), 271.

"Preparation for the Descent"

In his essay on Dante's *Divina Commedia*, Giorgio Agamben has written: *"The one who accomplishes the voyage of the Comedy is not a subject or an I in the modern sense of the word but, rather, simultaneously a* person *. . . and human* nature." Giorgio Agamben, *The End of the Poem* (Stanford: Stanford University Press, 1999), 20.

Testimony

This section, which portrays the *descent into hell* of contemporary war, does not refer to one geographic location or conflict. Some details that appear in it, however, were informed by the author's experience of attending witness sessions at an International Tribunal during the years 2002-2004.

The resemblance of these descriptions to other recent international events merely reflects the ubiquitious nature of torture and the view, articulated by the Polish poet Wisława Szymborska, that *"Nothing has changed . . . Tortures are just what they were, only the earth has shrunk / and whatever goes on sounds as if it's just a room away."*

(c) "When the illogical became the ferryman of the dead . . ." from personal notebooks 1999-2005.

"Testimony on What is Important"

Fragments of testimony presented in this poem, composed in *coblas unissonans*, come from a witness session at the International Criminal Tribunal for the Former Yugoslavia in The Hague, February 2001.

(d) "Do not hold it against me, O speech . . ." from Wisława Szymborska, *Miracle Fair* (New York: W. W. Norton & Company, 2001), 115.

"A Biography of Tyranny"

"A Biography of Tyranny" is dedicated to Anca Cristofovici.

Midnight dialogue

This section reflects upon the image of the *descent from the cross*, a moment understood in the context of this book as one of doubt and moral eclipse, or what the German critic Heinz Ickstadt has called "the bottom of history."

"On the Midnight Dialogue with History"

This poem is an imagined encounter with the figure of History at the beginning of the 21st century.

(e) "*. . . In what tense shall we now speak about the present . . .*" from personal notebooks 1999-2005.

"Twelve Reflections on Renewal"

In *The Human Condition*, Hannah Arendt writes: "*Without being forgiven, released from the consequences of what we have done, our capacity to act would, as it were, be confined to one single deed from which we could never recover . . . Only through this constant mutual release [...] can men remain free agents . . . trusted with so great a power as that to begin something anew.*" (Chicago: University of Chicago Press, 1958), 237, 240.

(f) "*The world is the closed door. It is a barrier. And at the same time it is the way through . . .*" from Simone Weil, *The Simone Weil Reader* (New York: David McKay Company, 1977), 119.

Update on the Descent explores three uses of the term "descent". Its three sections follow a HCANTCC pattern, alternating lyrics, aphorisms, anti-lyrics and philosophical notebooks.

The section *Testimony* is dedicated to Peter Fray of
The Canberra Times for his friendship.

I would like to express my gratitude to those individuals who gave
valuable criticism and support during the years when this book was written:
in the United States, L. S. and S. S.; in Paris, A. C., G. N. and T. P.;
in Ireland, K. and S. H.; in Germany, translator M. U.-P., and L. M.;
in Switzerland, N. F., D. J., U. H and J.-M. E.

With special gratitude to S. K. who gave me
un autre pays.

For M.

Index